SandCastle 2

More Blends

sl

Pam Scheunemann

ABDO
Publishing Company

Published by SandCastle™, an imprint of ABDO Publishing Company, 4940 Viking Drive, Edina, Minnesota 55435.

Printed in the United States.

Cover and interior photo credits: Artville, Corbis Images, Corel, Eyewire Images, FPG International, PhotoDisc, Stockbyte

Library of Congress Cataloging-in-Publication Data

Scheunemann, Pam, 1955-
    Sl / Pam Scheunemann.
       p. cm. -- (Blends)
     ISBN 1-57765-452-8
   1. Readers (Primary) [1. English language--Phonetics.] I. Title. II.
Blends (Series)
     PE1119 .S43517 2001
     428.1--dc21

                                                      00-056563

The SandCastle concept, content, and reading method have been reviewed and approved by a national advisory board including literacy specialists, librarians, elementary school teachers, early childhood education professionals, and parents.

Let Us Know

After reading the book, SandCastle would like you to tell us your stories about reading. What is your favorite page? Was there something hard that you needed help with? Share the ups and downs of learning to read. We want to hear from you! To get posted on the ABDO Publishing Company Web site, send us email at:

sandcastle@abdopub.com

Second printing 2002

About SandCastle™

Nonfiction books for the beginning reader

- Basic concepts of phonics are incorporated with integrated language methods of reading instruction. Most words are short, and phrases, letter sounds, and word sounds are repeated.

- Readability is determined by the number of words in each sentence, the number of characters in each word, and word lists based on curriculum frameworks.

- Full-color photography reinforces word meanings and concepts.

- "Words I Can Read" list at the end of each book teaches basic elements of grammar, helps the reader recognize the words in the text, and builds vocabulary.

- Reading levels are indicated by the number of flags on the castle.

Look for more SandCastle books in these three reading levels:

Level 1 (one flag)	**Level 2** (two flags)	**Level 3** (three flags)

Grades Pre-K to K 5 or fewer words per page	**Grades K to 1** 5 to 10 words per page	**Grades 1 to 2** 10 to 15 words per page

sl

Slade and his family have fun on the water slide.

sl

Sloane loves to hug her sleek kitty named Slinky.

sl

Sly is slim.

He likes to slurp his cereal.

sl

Mark slowly climbed the slender tree.

He did not slip.

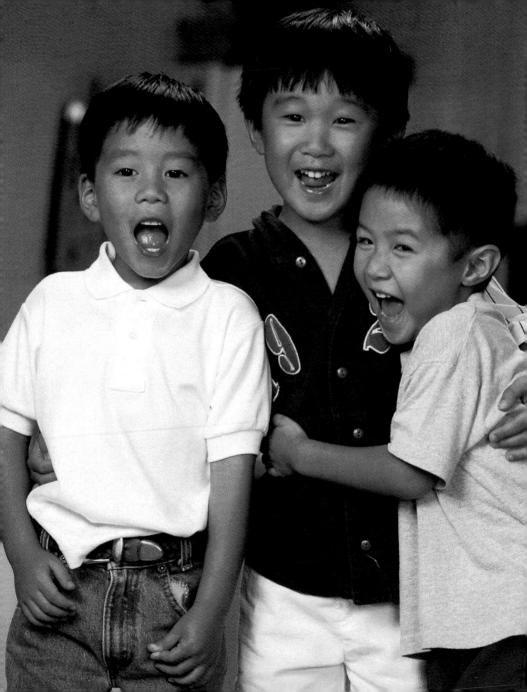

sl

Slane wears a rain slicker.

The weather is sloppy.

sl

Max sleds on the steep slope with his folks.

Words I Can Read

Nouns

A noun is a person, place, or thing

cereal (SIHR-ee-uhl) p. 9
family (FAM-uh-lee) p. 5
fun (FUHN) p. 5
kitty (KIT-ee) p. 7
slicker (SLIK-uhr) p. 17
slime (SLIME) p. 15

sling (SLING) p. 15
slope (SLOHP) p. 19
tree (TREE) p. 11
water slide (WAW-tur
  SLIDE) p. 5
weather (WETH-ur) p. 17

Plural Nouns

**A plural noun is more than one
person, place, or thing**

folks (FOHKSS) p. 19   pals (PALZ) p. 13

Proper Nouns

**A proper noun is the name
of a person, place, or thing**

Mark (MARK) p. 11
Max (MAX) p. 19
Rose (ROZE) p. 21

Slade (SLADE) p. 5
Slane (SLANE) p. 17
Slater (SLAY-tur) p. 13

22

sl

Max sleds on the steep slope with his folks.

sl

Rose is sly.

What is she pretending to do?

(sleep)

Words I Can Read
Nouns
A noun is a person, place, or thing

cereal (SIHR-ee-uhl) p. 9
family (FAM-uh-lee) p. 5
fun (FUHN) p. 5
kitty (KIT-ee) p. 7
slicker (SLIK-uhr) p. 17
slime (SLIME) p. 15

sling (SLING) p. 15
slope (SLOHP) p. 19
tree (TREE) p. 11
water slide (WAW-tur SLIDE) p. 5
weather (WETH-ur) p. 17

Plural Nouns
A plural noun is more than one person, place, or thing

folks (FOHKSS) p. 19

pals (PALZ) p. 13

Proper Nouns
A proper noun is the name of a person, place, or thing

Mark (MARK) p. 11
Max (MAX) p. 19
Rose (ROZE) p. 21

Slade (SLADE) p. 5
Slane (SLANE) p. 17
Slater (SLAY-tur) p. 13

Slinky (SLINK-ee) p. 7   **Sloane** (SLOHN) p. 7
Sloan (SLOHN) p. 15   **Sly** (SLYE) p. 9

Verbs

A verb is an action or being word

climbed (KLIMD) p. 11
did (DID) p. 11
do (DOO) p. 21
has (HAZ) p. 15
have (HAV) p. 5
hug (HUHG) p. 7
is (IZ) pp. 9, 13, 17, 21
likes (LIKESS) p. 9
loves (LUHVZ) p. 7
named (NAYMD) p. 7

pretending
 (pre-TEND-ing) p. 21
slaps (SLAPSS) p. 13
sleds (SLEDZ) p. 19
sleep (SLEEP) p. 21
slip (SLIP) p. 11
slipped (SLIPT) p. 15
slugs (SLUHGZ) p. 13
slurp (SLUHRP) p. 9
wears (WAIRZ) p. 17

Adjectives

An adjective describes something

her (HUR) p. 7
his (HIZ) pp. 5, 9, 13, 19
nice (NISSE) p. 13
rain (RAYN) p. 17
sleek (SLEEK) p. 7

slender (SLEN-dur) p. 11
slim (SLIM) p. 9
sloppy (SLOP-ee) p. 17
sly (SLYE) p. 21
steep (STEEP) p. 19

23

Match these sl Words to the Pictures

slice

sleep

slide

sled

24